# Paul Bunyan Moves Out

## by Destin Clark
## illustrated by Dave Blanchette

**Harcourt**

Orlando   Boston   Dallas   Chicago   San Diego

Visit *The Learning Site!*

**www.harcourtschool.com**

Sure, there have been some big babies. When I tell you about this one, though, you might change your mind about what big is.

Paul Bunyan was the biggest baby ever born. When he was two weeks old, he weighed one hundred pounds. His ma would walk around him, saying, "Oh, my!"

Paul was unusual in another way. He was born with a full head of hair. His ma could not use a regular comb to take care of it. The hair was too thick. So she got his pa to cut down a pine tree, and she used that to comb Paul's hair.

Feeding Paul was also a problem. When he woke up, wailing from hunger, he would eat six dozen eggs. For each egg, he ate a piece of bacon. He ate forty-five potatoes. By the time his ma finished feeding him breakfast, it was time for lunch. His ma needed all her wits to keep him fed.

Neighbors would come by to see how the giant baby was faring. They tried to give his ma advice on caring for him.

Meanwhile, Paul kept growing. When he was just a few months old, he rolled over in his sleep. He crushed four miles of trees and a small town. Luckily, the people all ran away before they got hurt.

"This is dreadful!" his ma exclaimed. "What can we do?"

Things got worse when Paul started to crawl. He was still a baby and didn't have the wits to be careful. By this time, he weighed over seven hundred pounds. When he crawled, he started an earthquake.

The people in the towns around Paul's home were not faring very well. "This is dreadful!" they all said. "That baby must leave. This place is too small for him!" Paul's parents understood why everyone was so upset, but they loved him too much to send him away.

The neighbors had some more advice for Paul's parents. "Make a boat for him, and put it in the sea. The waves will rock the boat like a cradle. Paul will be happy, and we will be safe."

His parents listened to the advice. They made a gigantic boat for Paul. At first, all was well.

Then Paul began to toss and turn in his sleep. The rocking of the boat sent giant waves crashing up on the beach.

The navy was called. It sailed out to tow Paul's cradle back to shore. When they got to shore, Paul woke up. He stepped out of his cradle and sank four ships.

Things got no better as Paul grew up. Finally, the neighbors came to talk to his parents again. "We're sorry," they said, "but Paul has got to make his home somewhere else." His parents agreed, but where could he go?

Paul's parents looked at maps. They found a place so far up north that no one had ever been there. "Paul," they said to him, "we'll take you there. Please carry us."

Paul tucked his parents into his shirt pocket, and off they went.

It took Paul just three hours to walk to his new home. "Be very careful," his parents told him. "Don't step on a village."

When the family got far enough to the north, Paul found a mountain. He scooped out enough earth to make a cave. With the earth he had scooped out, he made a new mountain.

"Here, son," said his father. "I made these for you." He handed Paul a giant ax, a giant fishing pole, and a giant knife.

His parents sadly told Paul farewell. "We'll miss you, honey," his ma said. "But we don't want anyone to get hurt."

"I understand," Paul said. "Farewell, Ma and Pa."

Paul was sad, even though he knew having his own home was for the best. He cried and cried for a month. He cried so much that he made a new river. When he heard a flopping sound, he stopped crying and sat up. There were fish in the river!

Paul got out his fishing rod and cast the line into the river. Soon he had dozens of fish piled up around him. Paul happily made a fire and cooked all of the fish for dinner. *This life will be all right after all*, he said to himself.

When Paul got tired of eating fish, he
learned to hunt moose. Soon, he started
exploring. Of course, he knocked down
many trees as he wandered around. Before
too long, he became known as the greatest
lumberjack of all time. Paul lived in the
North for many years. Some say he lives
there still!